GRIPPED BY A
GLOBAL GOD:
ONE GREATER THAN JONAH

SAMUEL H. LARSEN

xulon
PRESS

DEDICATION

To the honor of the One greater than Jonah whose unre-
lenting love sought and redeemed this errant sailor,

To my wife and covenant partner, Louise, who has
shared the storms, adventures, and joys of
our journey together, and

To our children and grandchildren, to whom we entrust
the future and God's legacy promised through
Jesus their Messiah.

CONTENTS

FOREWORD

Every people in every age has had its Nineveh—those people in the world to whom even the most evangelistic and fervent missionaries hesitate to go. Indeed when many Christians initially open their minds to consider wholly surrendering to God and following Him wherever He leads, there is often a check in their spirit. What if He calls me to be a missionary to *those* people in *that* place? Televisions and computer screens broadcast horrific news stories about the persecution of Christians in the hostile places of the world. Who would willingly walk into that trap? God called Jonah to go to such a place, and he ran.

The story of Jonah is a powerful story of how God brought a reluctant missionary to preach His word in the city of Nineveh, but it is so much more than that. It is a story that reflects the heartbeat of our missionary God. When searching for a biblical basis of missions, many turn their attention to the New Testament, and there is much there for them to find. However, the Bible resonates with God's passion for hopeless fallen people all the way through. In Genesis 3:15, God foretold the Good News promise of One who would come to destroy the work of the serpent, restoring them to Himself and giving hope for all who would follow. Although the Gospel in that passage is in shadow and can only be clearly seen by shining the light of the New Testament on it, it is there. Walking through the Old Testament reveals God's passion for the nations through the Law, the Writings, and the Prophets (cf. Genesis 12:3; Ruth; Psalm 67; Isaiah 49:6). As such, it is more accurate to say that there is really a missiological basis for the Bible than to say that there is a biblical basis for missions. The Bible teaches us what we need both to know God and to make Him known; that is what missions is all about.

Throughout history God has called men and women to reach and teach the nations. Yet sadly, still over one half of all the people groups in the world are counted as unreached, and just as tragic, many of those counted as reached are undiscipled people who often call themselves Christians, but who have no idea what it is to be a Christian or even who Jesus is. How can this be? We are a world of Jonahs. God has called men and women to the hard places who have often responded like Moses, "Here am I, send Aaron!" and people groups remain in darkness, bound in their pagan religions. Other missionaries were called to teach and disciple, but the harsh reality of life in those places or the difficult task of training Bible-less preliterate oral learners led them to choose places where their gifts might be used more effectively. No one can critique another's calling. The highest and best use of anyone's life is to do what God calls them to do in the place He calls them to do it. Yet, how else can we account for 2,000 years with the Great Commission and still one-third of the world's population, over one-half of the people groups, have never heard the Gospel?

In this insightful and instructive treatment of the Book of Jonah, Sam Larsen leads us on a journey into his world and heart; a journey where we meet ourselves along the way and are given an opportunity to consider all of these questions in light of the incredible story of God's plan for both Jonah and Nineveh. Dr. Larsen provides a marvelous illustration of the missiological hermeneutic. We would be greatly blessed to learn to read the Bible through a missionary lens, and to have our hearts beat with the heart of its Author. May we all learn Jonah's lesson of God's passion for the world's people and what our role is in His plan for the nations.

M. David Sills

ACKNOWLEDGMENTS

N o book writes itself, and this brief book is no exception.

The author is indebted to a host of others who have befriended him, worked alongside him, taught and mentored him, and tactfully offered him valuable criticism and correction. Students in seminary classes taught by the author over the years have, through their insightful questions, helped to refine the author's thinking and presentation. Faculty colleagues, including especially Professors Elias Medeiros, Dan Timmer, and Allen Curry, through their interaction with the author over the past decade, have helped to forge the main lines of the author's approach to the material. The staff at Xulon have been most supportive and helpful. Dr. Larry Keefauver's assistance with formulating the reflection and action suggestions at the end of each chapter has been invaluable. The "fingerprints" of many others as well are upon this book in ways both large and small, and the resulting work has much benefited from them all. Nevertheless, the author alone remains responsible for any errors in the book, and he simply offers it with humility as an all-too-fallible offering in service to his Lord.

May the Lord of the Harvest multiply the few loaves and fishes represented here that they may be used by Him to bring many to the true Bread and Water of Life.

INTRODUCTION

The Great Story of the Bible is punctuated by sub-plots that grip the imagination of even very young readers. As a young boy, I remember reading with bated breath the accounts of Noah's ark, of Moses parting the Red Sea, of Joshua at the walls of Jericho, of David the shepherd boy facing down the giant Goliath, of Daniel in the den of lions, and of Jesus walking on the water. So many more electrifying and inspiring stories are included within the book that is our Bible.

One that has always particularly intrigued me is the story of Jonah.

Personally, I found that I identified with Jonah. No, I have never been swallowed by a sea creature, nor has my preaching ever resulted in a city-wide revival. Yet something about Jonah's heart-condition and actions resonated with me. I asked myself,

- *How could he possibly have thought he could actually run away from God?*

- *What was he thinking?*
- *Moreover, why wouldn't he have rejoiced over the success of his (brief!) preaching stint?*

> *In this book, you will come to see the real* **superhero** *of the story – not Jonah, but the One who cares more than we do about coming to seek and to save that which was lost.*

Deep within my soul, I recognized that I, too, have run from the presence of the Lord. I, too, have had a value system in collision with God's heart. So the brief story of Jonah, wrapped as it is in the epic grand narrative of redemption, has a personal pull for me. Yet for years, I did not really understand it, at least in the context of redemptive history.

That is what this book is about—understanding the real back story, the behind-the-scenes drama and reality of Jonah's exciting life. I hope that you will enjoy reading it, and that you will share it, but His silhouette and behind-the-scenes actions envelop the story both of Jonah and the entire Bible.

Before beginning our journey together, in the interest of full disclosure, it is only fair to you, the reader, that your author acknowledge his own governing principles for exploring this wonderful, ancient, reality show in Scripture. Just so you know...

- **I believe the Bible was given by God through men upon whom God's Spirit rested for the purpose of revealing God's plan of salvation through Jesus Christ to us.** There are over forty authors; they wrote over a period of some fourteen hundred years.

- **The Bible is completely true, without error, and reliable for knowing God, and how we should live our lives according to His purpose.** Jesus clearly believed it to be so[1] and in the end I trust Jesus' judgment in the matter. Whole books have been published on this subject by more erudite scholars than I[2] and it is not the purpose of this short book to enter into that debate.

- **I also believe that God is not limited to what we ordinarily observe in the natural order of His creation and providence. God clearly has the ability to act miraculously within history and in our individual lives in ways that He deems wise and honoring to Him.** So, the flood of Noah, the parting of the Red Sea by Moses, the leveling of Jericho's massive bulwarks,

> *Miracles point beyond themselves to the power and purposes of God. They accredit the prophet and apostle in biblical times.*

the felling of the giant Goliath by a shepherd boy's sling stone, and the provision of a huge sea creature to swallow a runaway prophet are not obstacles to faith, but occasions for faith.

- That miracles do not happen routinely and are not commonplace is evident: their astounding and uncommon occurrence are an essential feature of why the Bible calls them miracles. But miracles are more than that; they point beyond themselves to the power and purposes of God. They accredit the prophet and apostle in biblical times.[3] Above all, they accredit the One of whom all the Law of Moses and the Prophets testified.[4] In the many stories within the Great Story of redemption, there are a gallery of heroes, but remarkably all are flawed— all save one. There is but one Hero of the Great Story, and all the subplots of the divine epic are woven together around Him.[5] We cannot rightly understand the story of Jonah unless we place that story within that larger context.

So journey with me to a land long ago, to become better acquainted with a much maligned and misunderstood prophet and deserter. You will uncover his life and times, and the place in God's Great Story which he fills. As you do, you may like me begin to trace out something of Jonah's likeness as you gaze honestly in the mirror.

But do not stop there. Keep searching the short storyline (just 48 verses) until you begin to see the implicit, mysterious, and awesome presence and activity of the promised One, the Messiah (God's Anointed). His character will quickly reveal His nature to you as so very different from yours, mine, and Jonah's. Messiah is altogether lovely. His great heart is filled with compassion for the multitudes and for the nations.[6] Come explore with me.

As you discover Jonah and read the biblical text, may God's Spirit whisper to you, "Behold your God!"

Map of Jonah's World

(Logos Bible Software. www.logos.com)

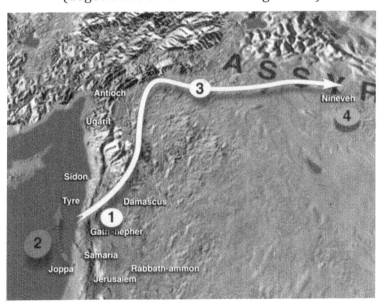

Chapter One

THE STAGE IS SET

J onah's story begins in a turbulent period of history. It was, in Dickens' terms, the best of times and the worst of times. To the prophet of God living in the northern kingdom of Israel, with its capital of Samaria, events likely appeared promising, even hopeful.

The Tide Turns

Upheaval marked the middle of the eighth century B.C. in the Fertile Crescent. Israel's nemesis and dominant neighbor, Syria, had been on the rise until the incursions of a greater power to Syria's east began to take its toll. Syria, with its capital at Damascus, was now in turn battered by conflict with the Assyrian empire, whose capitals alternated between Assur and Nineveh. Assyria's rise to power was as unstoppable as the Terminator's was in the popular films.

One by one, neighboring kingdoms fell to Assyrian armies. Never before had warfare been waged on such a scale, with siege engines and embankments reducing mighty walled defenses to rubble. The ancient world's ISIL or Taliban was Assyria. As a matter of state policy, the evil kingdom of Assyria used genocide and terror as a warning to all that resistance to Assyrian invasion would bring terrible retribution upon the whole population of any kingdom that dared refuse to submit. Cities that threw open their gates without resistance were spared, although their populations were systematically deported, and the conquered territories were then repopulated by deported people groups from other lands.

Part of the reason for this draconian tactic may have been to remove any hope of national resurgence under the patronage of the conquered people's territorial gods. An Assyrian chief official (the "rabsheka," or great sheikh) would, a century later, taunt Hezekiah and his people with the boast that the Lord was no more able to deliver Jerusalem than the gods of the people already conquered by Assyria. Isaiah, the prophet of God, records that account.[7]

In the middle of the eighth century, however, things suddenly changed. Damascus had indeed been badly weakened by the constant warfare with Assyria. Assyria, though, now herself entered a forty-year period of turbulence and disaster. Dynastic succession struggles threatened to tear apart the empire, and vassal kings seized the opportunity to escape the oppressive domination of their Assyrian overlords. The empire was fragmenting. To make matters worse, repeated droughts in Assyria brought famine, and when rains did come, they came in torrents, washing away the soil and bringing floods and plague upon the populace of Assur and Nineveh. Invasions by Scythians, a Mongol-related people, ravaged the land. Nineveh, in particular, was "on the ropes," as it were. Its proud armies were stretched thin and in tatters. Nineveh's legendary cruelty, not only toward conquered people and slaves, but even toward its own citizens, with the nobility's highhanded oppression of the common people, had reached a breaking point.

Jonah Arrives on the Scene

Enter Jonah. His name, which means "dove," carried with it biblical Hebrew associations with both peace, on the one hand, and foolishness, on the other.[8] He hailed from Gath-Hepher, a small town in Zebulon about five miles north of the site upon which the later town of Nazareth would be built. The vicinity of Gath-Hepher had been, and would be again, the route of invaders from the East. But Jonah's era was privileged.

A century earlier, God had anointed Jehu, an Israelite charioteer captain, to overthrow and destroy the dynasty of Ahab and his wicked Sidonian queen, Jezebel. Jezebel was notorious for her persistent efforts to stamp out

21

worship of the Lord and supplant it with the worship of the Sidonian Baal and his consort Asherah. The prophet Elijah contended with Ahab and the prophets of Baal at Mount Carmel. There Elijah had called down fire from heaven and had executed the false prophets of Baal. God pronounced judgment upon Ahab's dynasty.[9]

Jehu's energetic eradication of Ahab's line and of Baal worship brought him God's promise that his own dynasty would continue for four generations.[10] Jehu, however, failed to restore true worship of the Lord by removing the counterfeit temples, altars, and priests set up by the northern kingdom's first king, Jereboam the son of Nebat.[11] For his failure, his reign was marked by weakness and vassalage to foreign powers, first to Damascus and later to Assur. But God kept His promise nonetheless, and Jehu's line continued on the throne through his great-grandson, Jereboam II. It was in the reign of Jereboam II that Jonah served as prophet of God.

In the Court of Jereboam II

Jonah, like Elijah before him, seems to appear out of nowhere in the court of the king. Unlike Elijah, whose utterance was one of judgment in accordance with the warnings of God through His servant Moses as recorded in Deuteronomy, Jonah's message was undoubtedly popular and welcomed. The biblical narrative in 2 Kings gives this account:

In the fifteenth year of Amaziah son of Joash king of Judah, Jeroboam, son of Jehoash king of Israel became king in Samaria, and he reigned forty-one years. He did evil in the eyes of the LORD and did not turn away from any of the sins of Jeroboam son of Nebat, which he had caused Israel to commit. He was the one who restored the boundaries of Israel from Lebo Hamath to the Sea of the Arabah [the Dead Sea], in accordance with the word of the LORD, the God of Israel, spoken through his servant Jonah son of Amittai, the prophet from Gath Hepher. The LORD had seen how bitterly everyone in Israel, whether slave or free, was suffering; there was no one to help them.

And since the LORD had not said he would blot out the name of Israel from under heaven, he saved them by the hand of Jeroboam son of Jehoash. As for the other events of Jeroboam's reign, all he did, and his military achievements, including how he recovered for Israel both Damascus and Hamath, which had belonged to Yaudi [Judah], are they not written in the book of the annals of the kings of Israel? Jeroboam rested with his fathers, the kings of Israel. And Zechariah his son succeeded him as king.[12] (2 Kings 14:23-29)

King Zechariah would soon be deposed, but Jeroboam II would enjoy the longest reign of any of the kings of Israel. Jereboam II represented the fourth generation of Jehu's dynasty, and God was fulfilling His promise to Jehu given a century before. God not only preserved Jehu's dynasty through the reign of Jereboam, but God also granted Jereboam longevity, stability, and success. Israel, the northern kingdom, was still in rebellion against God by reason of their obstinate insistence on worship at their false sanctuary (by that time only the one at Bethel, as the one at Dan appears to have fallen out of use, perhaps due to invasions). Yet God graciously conferred upon the fourth generation of Jehu's royal house and upon Israel a wide-ranging renaissance—militarily, politically, economically, and artistically. There was, however, no spiritual renaissance of revival and reformation.

- *Was not the Lord Israel's God?*
- *And would not Israel's God defend His people against all who opposed them and were themselves outside His covenant?*
- *And as for the sanctuary at Bethel, had worship there not already continued for two hundred years?*
- *And yet had not the Lord continued to send His prophets to Israel and shown patience and favor toward their nation?*

They might not be the best worshipers of the true God, but they did not think they were so very bad, after all, especially compared to the foreign nations (the Gentiles) surrounding them. Surely God would not cast them aside; after all, they were all He had (excepting the rather smallish kingdom of David's dynasty, Judah, to the south). So, in one sense, they may have reasoned, *God owed them.*

Jonah's appearance and encouragement of Jeroboam was welcome, believed, and promptly acted upon. Why wouldn't God show favor to Israel?

Not all the prophets of God were altogether encouraging to the kingdom of Israel. Amos had prophesied against the nation for failing to return to the Lord, and he had spoken out directly against the

> *Jonah's agenda was not God's agenda!*

sanctuary at Bethel and its illegitimate high priest. Hosea, too, had warned of coming judgment on the kingdom, even alluding to exile in Assyria.[13] The prophets would have been well aware of one another's prophetic pronouncements: their messages, after all, came from one and the same Lord. So Jonah would have known of the prophecies of Amos and Hosea, but there is no indication that Jonah ever spoke a word of righteous rebuke at the court of Jeroboam. He may have enjoyed his role as the "patriot prophet." If so, God's agenda was not Jonah's.

Reclaiming the boundaries of David's kingdom (except for the southern kingdom of Judah under the continuing dynasty of David) would have taken some years to complete. Military campaigns were customarily conducted seasonally "at the time when kings go off to war,"[14] rather than being fought continuously year-round and for years on end. Jeroboam II reigned from 793-753 B.C. By the last quarter of his long reign, his military triumphs were likely complete. Many scholars would place the events of 2 Kings 14:25-27 somewhere near the mid-point of Jeroboam's reign.

The events of the book of Jonah itself may probably then be dated some time later (perhaps *circa* 760 B.C., as Gleason Archer has suggested).[15] If that date is accepted, then the Golden Age of the northern kingdom of Israel had only another ten years to run. Time was running out for Jereboam II and for Israel. Yet still there were no signs of spiritual renewal in either Israel or her king. The judgment announced by Amos and Hosea grew ominously more imminent. As far as Jonah was concerned, his agenda would collide with God's will and purposes in dramatic fashion. In fact, Jonah was about to enter a perfect storm!

Consider This...

- *How is the Northern Kingdom's response to God similar and different from America's response to God today?*

26

- *When your agenda differs from God's agenda for you, your family, and your culture, what do you do?*
- *If God is calling you to be like a Jonah today, what prophetic words might you have for America?*

Act Upon This...

- *Check the ways God wants to use you to become involved in bringing spiritual renewal to your family, church, community, region, and nation.*
  - Personal prayer and intercession.
  - Praying with a group of people regularly for spiritual renewal.
  - Becoming actively involved in living out and sharing God's Good News of peace through Jesus Christ in your family, neighborhood, classroom, or workplace.
  - Getting involved as a citizen politically to advocate for Judao-Christian (biblical) values in your community, state, or nation.
  - Joining a Christian organization that takes a public stand for Christ and biblical values. List the organizations your church recommends for your involvement and becoming a volunteer:

  _____

  _____

  _____

- Check off what keeps you from following God's agenda for your call or purpose in boldly and publically standing up for the Gospel in this culture:

  __Fear of rejection

  __Being ashamed of following Christ

  __Past guilt and sin

  __Lack of faith

  __Procrastination

  __Being uninformed or ignorant of ways the culture is rejecting God's ways.

  __Other:_____

- Write a prayer of repentance for following your own agenda instead of God's, asking for the boldness and courage to be salt and light in our culture for biblical values and declaring the Gospel:

  _____

  _____

  _____

Chapter Two

THE FUGITIVE

Jonah Flees From the Lord

The word of the LORD came to Jonah son of Amittai: "Go to the great city of Nineveh and preach against it, because its wickedness has come up before me." But Jonah ran away from the LORD and headed for Tarshish. He went down to Joppa, where he found a ship bound for that port. After paying the fare, he went aboard and sailed for Tarshish to flee from the LORD.

Then the LORD sent a great wind on the sea, and such a violent storm arose that the ship threatened to break up. All the sailors were afraid and each cried out to his own god. And they threw the cargo into the sea to lighten the ship. But Jonah had gone below deck, where he lay down and fell into a deep sleep. The captain went to him and said, "How can you sleep? Get up and call on your god! Maybe he will take notice of us, and we will not perish."

Then the sailors said to each other, "Come, let us cast lots to find out who is responsible for this calamity." They cast lots and the lot fell on Jonah. So they asked him, "Tell us, who is responsible for making all this trouble for us? What do you do? Where do you come from? What is your country? From what people are you?"

He answered, "I am a Hebrew and I worship the LORD, the God of heaven, who made the sea and the land."

This terrified them and they asked, "What have you done?" (They knew he was running away from the LORD, because he had already told them so.) The sea was getting rougher and rougher.

So they asked him, "What should we do to you to make the sea calm down for us?" "Pick me up and throw me into the sea," he replied, "and it will become calm. I know that it is my fault that this great storm has come upon you." Instead, the men did their best *to row back to land. But they could not, for the sea grew even wilder than before.*

Then they cried to the LORD, "O LORD, please do not let us die for taking this man's life. Do not hold us accountable for killing an innocent man, for you, O LORD, have done as you pleased."

Then they took Jonah and threw him overboard, and the raging sea grew calm. At this the men greatly feared the LORD, and they offered a sacrifice to the LORD and made vows to him. But the LORD provided a great fish to swallow Jonah, and Jonah was inside the fish three days and three nights. (Jonah 1:1–17)

Our story begins abruptly: "The word of the LORD came to Jonah son of Amittai." We have met Jonah before at the royal court of Jereboam II in Samaria. There he undoubtedly enjoyed the public recognition of a "patriot prophet," announcing the renaissance of Israel to heights not seen since the reigns of David and Solomon over the united kingdom before the division under Jereboam I, the son of Nebat. His prophecies of Israelite ascendance fulfilled, Jonah likely was known and respected throughout the kingdom and beyond, for Israel's success came at the expense of her neighbors. As Damascus and Nineveh sank into decline, their rulers and populations could scarcely have ignored the growing reputation of the prophet of the Lord on whose guidance King Jereboam II so successfully based his foreign and military policy.

Then our story takes one of its pivotal and unexpected turns: "Go to the great city of Nineveh and preach against it, because its wickedness has come up before me." *That command was the word of the Lord to Jonah.*

Jonah would have been stunned. To prophesy to his own people was to be expected. To prophesy against another people as part of an address to his own people was sometimes the mission of a prophet, primarily as encouragement or instruction to Israel. Actually to *go to a Gentile people* in order to prophesy a warning of impending judgment was nearly unheard of. Some have suggested that Jonah's reluctance sprang from his terror of what the Ninevites might do to him, or from his hatred for Gentiles in general. However, the narrative gives no hint of such fear or hatred. Jonah's interaction with Phoenician sailors would be evidence enough that his aversion to going to Nineveh was somehow different from his interaction with Gentiles in general.

Sparing Nineveh would mean eventual judgment upon Israel, whose national pride had soared with its fortunes, but whose spiritual condition had only deteriorated. The "patriot prophet" wanted none of that!

- *Why Nineveh?*
- *Why not Babylon or even Assur?*
- *Did not their sins cry out to heaven, and were they not also "great cities"?*

Jonah instinctively knew the answer. If God were determined to destroy Nineveh without hope for a reprieve, He would not have instructed His prophet to preach in person within it. Jonah's contemporary prophets to Israel, such as Amos and Hosea, had warned of God's coming judgment upon Israel, including exile in Assyria. So Jonah grasped intuitively that his mission implicitly extended hope to Nineveh, a call to national repentance, and throwing themselves upon the mercy of God. Sparing Nineveh would mean eventual judgment upon Israel, whose national pride had soared with its fortunes, but whose spiritual condition had only deteriorated. The "patriot prophet" wanted none of that.

Why Did Jonah Run?

Why did Jonah run? He knew that, unlike the pagan gods, the Lord had made the sky, the land, and the sea. Where could he possibly go to hide from the Lord?

It is not as though Jonah expected to get away with his escape. Rather, Jonah had a "God problem." If the Lord, as He had declared to Moses at Mount Sinai, was indeed a merciful and forgiving God, then if Nineveh were warned,

33

the city *might* just repent, and if they did, then God *might* spare them. That could result in the eventual fulfillment of Hosea's prophecy concerning Israel's exile to Assyria.

So, like Elijah a century earlier, Jonah "resigned." Elijah had gone to tender his resignation before the Lord at the place where Moses had stood when God declared His Name, having established His covenant with His people as a nation at Mount Sinai.[16] Jonah did not run *to* God, however, but *away from His presence.* If God were going to show mercy to Nineveh (and implicitly to bring eventual judgment upon Israel), then Jonah may have been determined that it would have to be through some other prophet. *He* would not be the instrument of such a plan.

> *He had raised his love for his people, a people whom God also loved, to a place before his love for God. At that point, Jonah's patriotism became idolatry.*

Why not just stay at home? Jonah seems not to have considered that option. Perhaps he remembered what had happened to Israel after Jericho had been destroyed under Joshua. One Israelite man, Achan, disobeyed God's prohibition against plundering the city, and his disobedience had brought down God's judgment upon the entire people of God.[17] So Jonah may have sought to put as much distance between himself and his beloved Israel as he could. He would not be the lightning rod of God's wrath. If he perished, he would at least not take Israel down with him. If that was indeed Jonah's motive, then he had raised his love for his people, a people whom God also loved, to a place *before* his love for God. At that point, Jonah's patriotism became idolatry.

Tempest at Sea

Jonah's flight comprised two stages: land and sea. He set out for the nearest large Gentile seaport, Joppa, which took him outside the territorial boundaries of Israel. There he found a ship bound for the opposite end of the known world from Nineveh: Tarshish. The Tarshish of Jonah's day was not the Tarsus in Asia Minor where the Apostle Paul grew up as part of the Jewish diaspora. The Tarshish toward which Jonah set sail lay near the Straits of Gibraltar in southern Spain (Iberia).

Whether Jonah actually expected his voyage would end well, we do not know. What we do know is that, exhausted, he went below deck and fell into such a deep slumber that the ship got underway and had traveled some distance when the storm overtook it. It was no ordinary storm. Yet Jonah slept on.

What can account for such a sleep?

True, Jonah had already journeyed some distance, probably on foot, to reach Joppa, but that length of journey was not so unusual in his day. He may have been tired, but such a deep sleep, for such a long period, and under such sea conditions, comes across as nearly a drunken or drugged stupor, and the text gives no hint of such conduct on Jonah's part. Rather, given the mission to which Jonah was now committed, abandoning his calling as prophet of the Lord and defying the Lord's command, he found himself derelict and in despair, resigned to God's eventual reckoning with him. Depression and hopelessness can bring with them, among other symptoms, a deep and soporific sleep that is a form of escape from reality. Such a resignation to his doom can readily account for Jonah's remarkable slumber.

Meanwhile, the sailors were struggling desperately to keep the ship afloat as the wind and waves pounded their little vessel. Their cargo, the delivery of which was essential for them to receive any recompense for their voyage, was cast over the side to lighten the ship so that she would not plough so heavily through the swells, taking water over the gunwales. The captain, perhaps looking for additional cargo or ship's tackle to jettison, went below deck. There he discovered Jonah, sound asleep. Surprised, he awakened Jonah with the plea that he do the only thing a non-sailor could do under the circumstances—pray to his god.

The captain, a Gentile pagan, would have known little of the Lord and not much more about his passenger (other than that he had paid the fare demanded for him to embark). He would have known nothing of another passenger asleep on the sea during a great tempest, who, when awakened, would still the storm, saying, "Peace! Be still!"[18] That passenger would grow up barely five miles from Jonah's hometown, near the Sea of Galilee. He would be named Jesus, but He would not be born for another seven and a half centuries. For his part, the captain of Jonah's ship was astounded that anyone could, or would, sleep under the conditions of such a storm.

Casting the Lot

There is no indication that Jonah prayed as the captain implored. Instead, it was left to the sailors to do so, each to his own god, pagan gods who could not deliver them. The sailors resorted to casting the lot, the only means they could think of that was available to them. The lot would not deliver them, but at least they hoped it would identify the culprit who had brought such supernatural catastrophe upon them. Now, casting lots aboard a heaving deck is no simple matter, but their attempt was successful. The lot managed to indicate a clear outcome: it fell on Jonah.

The sailors were already aware that this passenger was trying to get away from the god of his people. Such an action was not so unusual, perhaps, in their day. After all, pagan gods were mostly territorial deities with particular people groups devoted to their homage. To leave one's people and homeland was considered to be tantamount to leaving the jurisdiction of that god, who, after all, had rival deities in the territories and people groups in surrounding lands. No one may have raised an eyebrow at the answer their passenger had given them when they asked his business in wanting to embark on their ship.

However, in the midst of the storm, and with the lot accusingly identifying Jonah, that all changed. They asked him a rapid series of questions:

- *Who is responsible for making all this trouble for us?*
- *What do you do?*
- *Where do you come from?*
- *What is your country?*
- *From what people are you?*

Jonah's reply was succinct: "I am a Hebrew and I worship the LORD, the God of heaven, who made the sea and the land."

They were the more terrified, and asked him, "What have you done?"

They already knew that he was running from the Lord, but they did not know the circumstances. Had he taken something from his god's sanctuary? Had he committed sacrilege?

The tempest now grew impossibly tumultuous so they cut to the chase:

"What should we do to you to make the sea calm down for us?"

They may have expected him to tell them to return him to shore to face the judgment of his god. Perhaps they expected him to tell them to make some kind of sacrifice to Jonah's god. Instead, his answer stunned them with the most incredulous response!

Into the Depths

"Pick me up and throw me into the sea," he replied, "and it will become calm. I know that it is my fault that this great storm has come upon you."

Jonah's words did not evade guilt. They were a straightforward acknowledgment of his having brought calamity upon the sailors, who were innocent of Jonah's personal rebellion against God. What is surprising is that Jonah seems actually to have cared about the sailors, Gentile pagans as they were, enough to surrender his own life to save theirs. Saving Phoenician seamen, however, was not the same as saving Ninevites. The seamen presented no threat to the survival of his beloved Israel, as Nineveh did. Jonah was already resigned to his doom; this action while compassionate was not particularly courageous on Jonah's part. He was at that moment, as he would be again, ready to die.

Even more surprising is the reaction of the sailors. They were trapped because of the misdeed of their passenger, of which they had no prior knowledge. Yet they tried to row to shore in order, presumably, to remove him safely from the ship to the shore. Perhaps they truly cared for Jonah. Or perhaps they did not wish to run the risk of taking action against one upon whom a powerful god had determined to visit personal judgment. Pre-empting personal vengeance could bring down the wrath of a frustrated pagan deity upon the unwitting perpetrators. The sailors would have wanted no risk of that. We are not told their motives other than that they were afraid.

A ship at sea caught in a cyclonic storm system on the Mediterranean would not ordinarily be close enough to land to row for shore. Apparently Jonah's ship was close enough for land to be visible or for the sound of breakers near the shore to be heard. All

> *It is one of those rare previews of Pentecost that we see in the Old Testament, of Gentiles as Gentiles worshiping the Lord, the God of Israel. We are not told whether their conversions were genuine and lasting, and we never hear again of them – or do we?*

rowing was futile. The seas moved against the vessel, pushing it away from shore. Waves and currents may create counter flows that push objects away from shore.

Swimmers know of rip tides; sailors know of off shore currents.

In any event, the sailors had to give up. In the end, all they could do was to do as Jonah had directed. First they called out to Jonah's God, now actually naming him as the Lord, God's covenant Name, and asking him not to hold them responsible for the death of an innocent man, since the Lord had done as He pleased.

Jonah was scarcely over the side and vanished from view when the sea suddenly became calm. Likewise, nearly eight centuries later, Galilean fishermen in their boat on the Sea of Galilee would experience a similar episode, and they too would be afraid, a fear provoked by the sudden calm, a fear even greater than their terror of the tempest.

These Gentile sailors had understandably been afraid of the storm. They had been even more terrified when Jonah told them who he was and why he was running. Yet at the unexpected and abrupt calm that so immediately followed Jonah's disappearance, we are now told that they "greatly feared the LORD, and they offered a sacrifice to the LORD and made vows to him." Sometimes deliverance instills more reverential fear than the circumstances from which we are delivered.

So also would the Galilean fishermen fear when Jesus stilled the storm, declaring of Jesus: "Who is this, that even the winds and the waves obey him?"[19] The Galileans, however, were at least Israelites. The Phoenician sailors were

Gentile pagans. They would hardly have known how to pray to the Lord, how to sacrifice to Him, or how to make vows pleasing to Him. Yet that is what they did. It is one of those rare previews of Pentecost that we see in the Old Testament, of Gentiles *as Gentiles* worshiping the Lord, the God of Israel. We are not told whether their conversions were genuine and lasting, and we never hear again of them – or do we?

Where was Jonah when the sea grew calm? He had slipped beneath the waves, fully expecting to drown, crying out in his heart to the Lord for deliverance from a watery death. He was not on deck to witness all that happened afterward—the sudden great calm, the fear of the sailors, their sacrifices, and vows.

- *How would Jonah know of those details which he included in the book that bears his name?*
- *Is it possible that God simply gave the knowledge by special revelation to another prophet who wrote the book?*

More likely, either Jonah himself, or his later scribe or disciple (as Baruch was to Jeremiah), wrote the book.

As we shall see, the events of chapter two could only have been known to Jonah and to God. The sailors, however, would have returned to port immediately. We can safely surmise that action on their part based upon the fact that the ship was battered and its tackle jettisoned.

The vessel had no reason to continue onward all the way to Tarshish without a cargo to deliver. They would have returned home as quickly as they were able. They would have brought with them the tale of a storm and of a strange prophet, whose identity would only add to his international notoriety thereafter.

Meanwhile, God had already provided a great sea creature (Hebrew, "*dag gadhol*") to swallow Jonah. It was a three-day and three-night "time out" for the wayward prophet of God. There would be nothing for him to do but to remember, reflect, meditate, and pray.

Consider This...

- Jonah found himself derelict and in despair, resigned to God's eventual reckoning with him. Depression and hopelessness can bring with them, among other symptoms, a deep and soporific sleep that is a form of escape from reality.
  Have you tried to run away from something God has called you to do and then found yourself in a situation like this?

- Sometimes deliverance instills more reverential fear than the circumstances from which we are delivered.
  Have you experienced a rescue that only God could have done and then felt reverential fear?
  What does reverential fear mean to you?

Act Upon This...

- Jonah's words did not evade guilt.
  When you have knowingly moved away from God and His direction for your life, go to Him and confess the truth of what you have done.
  Do your words try to evade guilt by making excuses for why you did what you did?

- "Go to the great city of Nineveh and preach against it, because its wickedness has come up before me."
  Has God told you to go into an area and preach the gospel or preach against the evil and wickedness? Have you obeyed? Why or why not?

- To *go to a Gentile people* in order to prophesy a warning of impending judgment was nearly unheard of.
  Has God called you to do something nearly unheard of?
  Explain:

- Jonah grasped intuitively that his mission implicitly extended hope to Nineveh, a call to national repentance, and throwing themselves upon the mercy of God. The "patriot prophet" wanted none of that. Jonah had a "God problem."
  Do you have a "God problem"?

Do you feel the person or persons to whom God is sending you do not deserve God's mercy?
How much mercy has God extended to you?

- It was a three-day and three-night "time out" for the wayward prophet of God. There would be nothing for Jonah to do but to remember, reflect, meditate, and pray.
  Has God ever put you in an extended "time out"?
  What did you learn during that time?

Chapter Three

GOD'S CAPTIVE

Jonah's Prayer

From inside the fish Jonah prayed to the LORD *his God. He said:*

"In my distress I called to the LORD, *and he answered me. From the depths of the grave I called for help, and you listened to my cry. You hurled me into the deep, into the very heart of the seas, and the currents swirled about me; all your waves and breakers swept over me. I said, 'I have been banished from your sight; yet I will look again toward your holy temple.' The engulfing waters threatened me, the deep surrounded me; seaweed was wrapped around my head. To the roots of the mountains I sank down; the earth beneath barred me in forever. But you brought my life up from the pit, O* LORD *my God.*

When my life was ebbing away, I remembered you, Lord, and my prayer rose to you, to your holy temple. Those who cling to worthless idols forfeit the grace that could be theirs. But I, with a song of thanksgiving, will sacrifice to you. What I have vowed I will make good. Salvation comes from the Lord."

And the Lord commanded the fish, and it vomited Jonah onto dry land. (Jonah 2:1–10)

Jonah was losing consciousness, his life was ebbing away. The waters were deep enough to overwhelm him, especially as the mighty waves created undertows that pulled him down. The sailors had vainly rowed for shore, so the ship would not have necessarily been in deep water, but it was deep enough. The sudden calm on the surface of the deep would not have helped Jonah, for he was now entangled in the rope-like bonds of seaweed, perhaps a form of kelp forest rising from the seafloor. The seamount beneath him was rugged, and the currents swirled around him. He found himself hopelessly entangled and lodged between the crevasses at the foot of the seamounts as they rose toward the surface.

Jonah's situation seemed utterly hopeless. The consequences of his attempt to run from God were now immediate and real. Jonah's last conscious thought was a cry of desperation to the Lord for deliverance.

Creature from the Deep

In the stormy, mud and debris filled water, at a depth where only the dimmest light pierced the swirling sea, and with seaweed covering his face, Jonah would not have seen it coming. He could have done little about it in any case. He was unable to free himself from the rocky rift into which the current pressed him, and he was by now nearly, perhaps entirely, unconscious. Dark and monstrously large, a creature from the deep approached with sudden speed. In the blink of an eye, Jonah was sucked into the maw of the monster. Somehow he lodged within it at a place where he was not enveloped by the strong gastric digestive fluids of the animal's stomach and intestines. Remarkably, there was breathable air, though the stench may have been powerful. There Jonah recovered consciousness.

> Jonah's song concludes with the powerful statement of faith: "Those who trust in worthless idols forfeit the grace that could be theirs. Salvation belongs to the Lord."

Jonah did not know it was a whale. Indeed, Jonah did not recount it as a whale in his narrative. What he does record is that it was a *dag gadhol*, a great sea creature, and that the Lord had especially prepared it for just this moment. Jonah's God had not been caught off guard by events as they unfolded; rather, He orchestrated them. He had hurled the great wind and the storm, He had caused the sailors' lot to fall upon Jonah, and He had prepared whatever Leviathan it was that lurked, waiting for a meal, as Jonah sank to the seafloor and became lodged between the rocks at the base of the seamount. Jonah's desperate prayer was heard by a God who answers before His loved ones call upon Him, and who hearkens while they are still imploring Him. [20]

In God's Custody

Jonah had three days and three nights to think, remember, reflect, pray, and resolve. It was a necessary retreat into isolation for the fugitive prophet, who now found himself, on the one hand, saved from a watery grave, and on the other hand, captive within the interior, somewhere, of a creature whose form he could not see but could only imagine.

We may wonder how Jonah knew how much time was passing by. He was experiencing a form of sensory deprivation, with no ordinary clues in his environment to cue him to the regular passage of time. He may only have realized how long he had been there after he emerged from the creature and interacted once more with other human beings on land. He would not have had, within the creature, any light by which to see, nor book from which to read, nor quill, ink, and parchment with which to write. His song, for that is what it was, was a prayer from the heart that he crafted and polished as he awaited the consummation of his salvation from the depths.

The creature was the instrument of God's saving him from death and of bringing the fugitive into custody, but the creature was not his final deliverance: that would be his being able once again to fulfill his vows to the Lord at Solomon's temple on Mount Zion in Jerusalem. Solomon's temple remained officially off limits to citizens of the northern kingdom, who were still being diverted by Israel's kings to worship instead at their counterfeit temple, altar, and priests at Bethel. Jonah knew the Lord, and he knew well that the Lord had chosen Zion as His sanctuary. It would be at the temple in Zion that Jonah would fulfill his vows.

Jonah's Song

Jonah had no library with him in the gullet of the creature, no topical concordance by which to find Scripture passages relevant to his situation. But he had time to think and to remember. He had steeped his mind in the Word of God, memorizing and meditating upon it,

> *It is sometimes said that if God wants you to do something for him, and you refuse to do it, he will simply do it using someone else. One wonders how Jonah would have replied to such an assertion.*

and now the Spirit of God brought those verses back to his mind. They convicted him, and they encouraged him. Most of all, they gave him hope and assurance that God was not finished with him yet.

Jonah's prayer virtually breathes the Scriptures, especially the Psalms. His prayer is a song (as were the Psalms themselves) of confession of his helplessness and hopelessness, and a recounting of his cry to God for help. His song concludes with the powerful statement of faith: "Those who trust in worthless idols forfeit the grace that could be theirs. Salvation belongs to the Lord."

In that last sentence, Jonah sums up the center of what would become the central point of his book. In the Hebrew language of Jonah's people, it is the name of Jesus: "The LORD Saves."[21] Indeed, the experience of Jonah would become a sign by which Jesus would, nearly eight centuries later, describe as symbolic of His own redemptive mission.

Deliverance

Jonah's lesson learned, the prophet, disciplined and humbled, was ready to resume his service to God. The text of the narrative is brief: "The LORD spoke to the sea creature, and it vomited Jonah upon the dry land."

Fresh air! Sunlight! Access to food and fresh water! The prospect of a bath and a change of clothes—all those must have seemed anything but ordinary to the prophet.

Now he could fulfill the vows he had made. His rebellious will had been broken. His faith in his God had not been crushed, but was rather strengthened. Perhaps Jonah's skin and hair were forever bleached and patchy, marks of one who had been confined to the belly of a monstrous sea creature. If so, his appearance would have added to the legends being told about him by the sailors after their return to port. His notoriety would likely have been greater than before.

It is sometimes said that if God wants you to do something for Him, and you refuse to do it, He will simply do it using someone else. One wonders how Jonah would have replied to such an assertion. Perhaps you have heard the adage: "If not me, who? If not now, when? If not here, where?" Certainly, God can use someone else; yet Jonah's story may put into question such a simplistic answer. Perhaps Jonah's story suggests that when God has the right person, at the right time, for the right task, then God may move all of nature to push that person in the right direction. God is not surprised by your immediate obedience or by your running away. But you may be surprised by how He responds to your attempt at avoiding or delaying His plan for you!

Jonah still did not have a complete answer to his God problem, but he was certain that there was an answer and that he could trust God with it. He did not have to have all the answers to his theological dilemma in order to acknowledge the Lord as his God. He was now a vessel in waiting for his Lord's command.

Consider This...

It is sometimes said that if God wants you to do something for Him, and you refuse to do it, He will simply do it using someone else. One wonders how Jonah would have replied to such an assertion.

- *Do you believe if God has called you to do something for Him that if you refuse He will simply get someone else to do it?*
- *Has there been a time in your life that God has allowed difficult circumstances to turn you around from rebellion to repentance?*
- *Explain your answer:*

Act Upon This...

Jonah still did not have a complete answer to his God problem, but he was certain that there was an answer and that he could trust God with it.

- *Do you believe you can trust God with whatever problem you are facing right now in your life?*
- *Why or why not?*

Jonah realized he did not have to have all the answers to his theological dilemma in order to acknowledge the Lord as his God.

- *Do you feel you have to have all the answers to your questions in order to do what God has called you to do?*
- *Why or why not?*

Jonah was now a vessel in waiting for his Lord's command.

- *Does this describe you? When God commands, how will you respond? And will your response be reluctant or eager...procrastinating or prompt?*

Chapter Four

AT NINEVEH

Jonah Goes to Nineveh

Then the word of the L*ORD* *came to Jonah a second time:*

"Go to the great city of Nineveh and proclaim to it the message I give you."

Jonah obeyed the word of the L*ORD* *and went to Nineveh. Now Nineveh was a very important city—a visit required three days. On the first day, Jonah started into the city.*

He proclaimed: "Forty more days and Nineveh will be overturned."

The Ninevites believed God.

They declared a fast, and all of them, from the greatest to the least, put on sackcloth.

When the news reached the king of Nineveh, he rose from his throne, took off his royal robes, covered himself with sackcloth and sat down in the dust. Then he issued a proclamation in Nineveh:
"By the decree of the king and his nobles:
Do not let any man or beast, herd or flock, taste anything; do not let them eat or drink. But let man and beast be covered with sackcloth. Let everyone call urgently on God. Let them give up their evil ways and their violence. Who knows? God may yet relent and with compassion turn from his fierce anger so that we will not perish."
When God saw what they did and how they turned from their evil ways, he had compassion and did not bring upon them the destruction he had threatened.
(Jonah 3:1–10)

We are not told how much time elapsed between Jonah's being unceremoniously deposited upon the shore and receiving God's call the second time. It may have been very soon thereafter, or it may have been weeks or even months as Jonah made his pilgrimage to Solomon's Temple in Jerusalem, capital of the southern kingdom of Judah. Jonah had promised to fulfill his vows at God's Temple, and Jonah would not have regarded the king's shrine at Bethel as legitimate. God's commandments through Moses required all able-bodied Israelite men to present themselves before God at His sanctuary three times each year at the feasts of Passover, Pentecost, and Tabernacles. Perhaps Jonah carried out his promise at one such feast. Or, God may have delayed Jonah from immediately carrying out his vow, instead giving the prophet a renewed call to preach at Nineveh. We are simply told, "The word of the LORD came to Jonah a second time: Go to the great city of Nineveh and proclaim to it the message I give you."

A Change of Heart?

This time, the prophet's response was different. We read, "Jonah obeyed the word of the LORD and went to Nineveh." Are we to envision the prophet as still inwardly unwilling, but simply coerced into reluctant and resentful compliance? Probably not, but we are not told what the prophet thought or felt—only that he obeyed and went. The combination of the terms "obeyed and went" is significant, however. It would have been enough, had the prophet still been recalcitrant in heart, to say that he "went." The narrative instead tells us that Jonah both "obeyed" and "went." The implication seems to be that

> *The combination of the terms "obeyed and went" is significant. The implication seems to be that his inward intentions as well as his outward actions were both in accordance with the commandment of God.*

his inward intentions as well as his outward actions were both in accordance with the commandment of God. If so, then Jonah had learned at least part of the lesson God intended to teach him. A further lesson still lay before him.

The message Jonah dutifully heralded in Nineveh was one of impending judgment: "Forty more days and Nineveh will be overturned." On the surface of it, the message was one purely of doom, with no explicit offer of any possibility of reprieve. One would have thought such a message would be agreeable to Jonah's hope for elimination of a future conqueror of his beloved homeland.

However, Jonah must have suspected a different outcome. He knew the character of Israel's God—the Lord forgives, and is "gracious and compassionate, slow to anger and abounding in love, a God who relents from sending calamity."[22] There was always the possibility that the Ninevites would repent and that God might spare them. Jonah could not control their responses. He could only do as he had been told.

Unexpected Response

The city of Nineveh comprised four urban centers within a greater metropolitan area. To stop at only the most prominent and frequented centers of government and commerce would have taken a good three days of walking and then preaching, even with his very brief message. His message was not a sermon, but rather more of an abrupt proclamation. Jonah had only just begun to preach in the city when his preaching was pre-empted. The response was surprising and spectacular. A wave of fear and remorse swept through the populace. It was a grassroots movement that quickly spread to include all socio-economic and political classes.

Some might dismiss the Ninevites' response as merely an ancient example of mass hysteria. Jesus would later say that they "repented." It was more than mere mass hysteria; it was sustained, and it included a change in the way the people lived and treated one another.

What kind of repentance was it? The references to God in the narrative use the general term for God normally used in contexts involving Gentiles. There is no record of the Ninevites relating to God by using His covenant name, the Lord. There is no historical record of any center of worship of the Lord in Assyria during the middle of the eighth century B.C.

There is temporal repentance, and then there is true repentance. The term signifies *turning*—going in the opposite direction. It is possible to "turn" temporarily from sinful conduct without having a changed heart that will persevere out of a profound personal experience of the grace of God. "Foxhole conversions" are notorious examples of temporal repentance that do not last beyond the danger or extreme need in which the subjects find themselves.

Biblical examples of such temporal repentance include Pharaoh in his dealing with the Hebrew slaves in Egypt, and of Saul in his dealing with David, whom he feared and of whom he was jealous. In the cases of Pharaoh and of Saul, the temporal repentance did not last. Yet wicked King Ahab, upon hearing the announcement of God's impending judgment upon his family line, humbled himself publicly before God, and God took notice giving him a reprieve for the time being. So, this temporary repentance by Nineveh would bring some relief from the ultimate judgment of God.

Nineveh would receive such a reprieve and would eventually emerge again as a conquering world power. Just as Ahab's life did not continue in repentant submission to God, so the Ninevites soon returned to their old ways. As God's judgment had fallen upon both Ahab and his dynasty, so prophets like Nahum would pronounce God's eventual judgment upon Nineveh. Assyria would be crushed to rise no more, but that day would come a century too late to save Israel.

Converts?

Eight centuries after Jonah, the Apostle Paul would declare that the inclusion into the family of the God of Abraham of Gentile believers *as Gentiles*, without their first becoming assimilated into the Jewish people, was a mystery not revealed until his day. By "mystery," Paul did not mean a puzzle to be solved or guessed, but a reality that could never be guessed or reasoned out by human beings or angels. It could only be known by God revealing it.

> *There is temporal repentance, and then there is true repentance. The term signifies turning. It is possible to "turn" temporarily from sinful conduct without having a changed heart that will persevere out of a profound personal experience of the grace of God.*

That Gentiles might be drawn to the God of Abraham was well attested, and there were many examples recorded in the Hebrew Scriptures. They were, however, as a rule expected to undergo the covenant rite of circumcision and then be incorporated into Israel as Jewish proselytes. The experience of the church of Antioch recorded in the New Testament book of Acts, in which Gentiles would be received as full-fledged members of the covenant community, would only arise eight centuries after Jonah. Calvary and Pentecost lay between the two events.

In Nineveh, news of the prophet's message and of the popular response reached the king. Together with his nobles, the king issued a proclamation. The inclusion of the nobles is an indication both of solidarity and probably also of the king's weakened political primacy during what one scholar has called the "forty lean years" of Assyria.[23]

The people had spontaneously proclaimed a fast. The king and his nobles made it official, and took it a step further, spelling out the terms of the fast. Those terms seem draconian to us today, and one can hardly imagine keeping water as well as food from human infants as well as animals for very long.

It may be that the fast was not intended to last the full forty days until the threatened disruption of the city, but only until they attracted the attention of God. Such a practice would be in keeping with their previous pagan ways of entreating their gods. We simply do not know due to the brevity of the narrative.

We do know that the king called upon the people unconditionally to demonstrate grief, humility, and changed behavior, saying, "Who knows? God may yet relent and with compassion turn from his fierce anger so that we will not perish." Their repentance constituted no guarantee that God would be compelled to relent. Rather, their hope was in the graciousness of God. There is no mention of sacrifice, or of vows, or of declaration that the Lord alone would be worshiped as their God. Even so, while not incontrovertibly evidencing conversion, their actions conveyed at least temporal repentance, and God took note.

Some have suggested that a mass movement among the populace of such a huge city could hardly have occurred so quickly. Given the historical context the reaction of the Ninevites is quite credible. Considering the duress caused by dynastic succession struggles, drought, famine, floods, plague, the Scythian invasion, Jonah's notoriety, and looking as he likely did as one back from the grave might account for this mass movement. If Jonah's brief message had been immediately accompanied by a total eclipse of the sun, which actually occurred at Nineveh on June 15, 763 BC, a mass hysteria may have accompanied the Ninevites' response and leant it even more urgency.

Without doubt, however, more than the orchestration of the historical context, the convicting work of the Spirit of God must be credited with the people movement of repentance. Although it appears it was not a repentance unto faith in the Lord, but only a belief in the warning of God, their temporal repentance was the result of the Spirit of God. God's Spirit was restraining evil in the world while preparing the way for the coming of the promised Son of David, the Redeemer of His people.

Reprieve

The final verse of Jonah chapter three tells us: "When God saw what they did and how they turned from their evil ways, he had compassion and did not bring upon them the destruction he had threatened." The note of hope implicitly conveyed in the explicit warning of impending judgment was grounded upon the character of God. Through the prophet Jeremiah, He would later declare,

"If at any time I announce that a nation or kingdom is to be uprooted, torn down and destroyed, and if that nation I warned repents of its evil, then I will relent and not inflict on it the disaster I had planned."[24]

Nineveh had been spared. Its moment of greatest vulnerability and imminent danger had passed. Within a generation, it would again be a capital of a resurgent Assyria, as ruthless as ever and intent upon expansion and world conquest. Jonah's great fear would be realized as Samaria would be destroyed and Israel would be carried into captivity—by the very people whose destruction he had helped to avert with his proclamation of God's warning. Still, Jonah in this experience was to learn more about himself and God's character as we shall now see.

Consider This...

There is *temporal repentance*, and then there is *true repentance*. The term signifies turning. It is possible to "turn" temporarily from sinful conduct without having a changed heart that will persevere out of a profound personal experience of the grace of God.

What is the difference between true repentance and temporal repentance?

"Foxhole conversions" are notorious examples of temporal repentance that do not last beyond the danger or extreme need in which the subjects find themselves.

How would you define a foxhole conversion?
Have you ever had a foxhole conversion?
Explain your answer.

Act Upon This...

If you have not fully repented of something you know God is not pleased with, do not hesitate. Truly repent and turn away from the sin and turn toward God. One cliché with some merit about repentance goes like this: *Admit it. Quit it. Forget it.* In other words, true repentance is not simply a temporary turning seeking relief from God's judgment. Once sin is confessed, true repentance moves into both no longer doing what is wrong and beginning to do what is right. Then, one's heart can truly release the past with its condemnation, and walk in the freedom of God's grace and forgiveness. This moment is there unconfessed and hidden sin in your heart? If so, complete the following:

Lord Jesus Christ, I confess _____
_____.

Lord Jesus Christ, I will quit _____
_____.

Lord Jesus Christ, I will start doing the right action of ____

_____.

If possible, I will also make restitution to the person(s) I sinned against by _____.

Lord Jesus Christ, I will no longer walk in condemnation, but in Your Spirit of grace and forgiving love, and I will testify about You that _____.

Also, like Jonah, make sure you obey and then go and do what God has told you to do.

> *Are your inward intentions as well as your outward actions both in accordance with the commandment of God?*

> *To whom will you be accountable to walk in repentance, humility, holiness, and fear of the Lord in the future?* _____

Chapter Five

SEVERE MERCY

Jonah's Anger at the Lord's Compassion

But Jonah was greatly displeased and became angry.
He prayed to the LORD, "O LORD, is this not what I said
when I was still at home?
That is why I was so quick to flee to Tarshish. I knew
that you are a gracious and compassionate God, slow
to anger and abounding in love,
a God who relents from sending calamity.
Now, O LORD, take away my life, for it is better for me
to die than to live."
But the LORD replied, "Have you any right to be angry?"
Jonah went out and sat down at a place east of the
city. There he made himself a shelter, sat in its shade
and waited to see what would happen to the city.
Then the LORD God provided a vine and made it

grow up over Jonah to give shade for his head to ease his discomfort, and Jonah was very happy about the vine. But at dawn the next day God provided a worm, which chewed the vine so that it withered. When the sun rose, God provided a scorching east wind, and the sun blazed on Jonah's head so that he grew faint.

He wanted to die, and said, "It would be better for me to die than to live."

But God said to Jonah, "Do you have a right to be angry about the vine?"

"I do," he said. "I am angry enough to die."

But the LORD said, "You have been concerned about this vine, though you did not tend it or make it grow. It sprang up overnight and died overnight. But Nineveh has more than a hundred and twenty thousand people who cannot tell their right hand from their left, and many cattle as well. Should I not be concerned about that great city?" (Jonah 4:1–11)

Our recalcitrant prophet had obeyed. He had duly done as he had been commanded. He had preached impending judgment to the populace of one of the most wicked ancient cities that had existed up to his day. Then, when Jonah had hardly begun to preach, the totally unexpected happened. A wave of fear and remorse swept over the city. It began with the grass roots and reached the ears of the king. They changed their behavior, humbled themselves, and pled for mercy from God. How many preachers today long to see such a movement of God's Spirit follow their proclamation of God's Word? Perhaps most, but...

Not Jonah. The text tells us he was unhappy about it. In fact he was more than unhappy, he was *greatly displeased.* His internalized value system, his personal and prejudiced expectations were violated, and it mattered very much to him. He became *angry.*

> Jonah's outburst betrays his sentiments in an agitated prayer to the Lord. God's reply is simply one question, "Have you any right to be angry?"

Now, there is anger, and there is **anger**, i.e. sinful fury, or wrath! God is described at times as angry. God's anger is always consistent with His holiness. Jesus was angry, too, at times. Our Lord was indignant with His own disciples when they sought to "protect" His time from interruptions by young mothers with their nursing infants.[25] Jesus rebuked them and used the occasion to teach a powerful lesson about membership in the Kingdom of God.

Once at the beginning and once at the end of His public ministry, Jesus purged the Temple court (probably the court of the Gentiles or outer precincts, which was as far as non-Jews were permitted to approach the sacred

Temple court itself, with its altar and water basin).[26] Jesus overturned the tables of the money-changers and drove out the animals brought in for sale, and He did so with a scourge in His hand. His disciples remembered afterward the scripture, "Zeal for your house has consumed me."[27] He was not serene in His actions or demeanor on those occasions.

At another time, a man with a shriveled hand was present while Jesus was in a synagogue on the Sabbath. His enemies, looking for a reason to accuse Him, waited to see if He would heal on the Sabbath.

> *Then Jesus asked them, "Which is lawful on the Sabbath: to do good or to do evil, to save life or to kill?" But they remained silent. He looked around at them in anger and, deeply distressed at their stubborn hearts, said to the man, "Stretch out your hand." He stretched it out, and his hand was completely restored. Then the Pharisees went out and began to plot with the Herodians how they might kill Jesus.* (Mark 3:4-6)

God was angry with Moses[28] when Moses tried to avoid God's calling to be an instrument of deliverance for the Hebrew slaves. The Scriptures tell us, "God is angry with the wicked every day."[29]

Followers of Jesus are told, "'In your anger do not sin': Do not let the sun go down while you are still angry, and do not give the devil a foothold."[30]

God's wrath is always holy, just, and measured; ours often is not. The instances in Jesus' ministries when He expressed righteous indignation all seem to have one feature in common. It was never because Jesus was being personally maligned, but when the helpless and vulnerable were being prevented from coming to God for healing or for blessing.

So, it is possible to be moved by a holy anger. If we are honest, we will probably have to admit that most of our own anger is *not* holy, even if it has a thread of principle behind which we may mask our more selfish motives. We are not so different from Jonah after all. We often feel like God should stop or even punish or destroy our enemies. We conveniently forget Jesus' mandate: *love your enemies.*

Jonah's anger was not motivated by zeal for God's holy name and His revealed purpose for the nations. He cared deeply for his own people, a people whom God had chosen and through whom God had promised the coming Son of David. That God could relent from carrying out catastrophic judgment on wicked Nineveh, regardless of any turning by its king and people, and through that same city bring judgment upon spiritually unresponsive Israel was too much for the patriot prophet to bear. *He fumed.*

Jonah's outburst betrays his sentiments in an agitated prayer to the Lord:

> *"O LORD, is this not what I said when I was still at home? That is why I was so quick to flee to Tarshish. I knew that you are a gracious and compassionate God, slow to anger and abounding in love, a God who relents from sending calamity. Now, O LORD, take away my life, for it is better for me to die than to live."*

God's reply is simply one question, "Have you any right to be angry?"

Jonah does not answer. He simply moves to a vantage point east of the city to watch what would now become of Nineveh. He may have thought to himself, "Perhaps their 'foxhole conversion' will not last a week, let alone forty days." Selfishness, greed, and old habits would surely reassert themselves, Jonah may have reasoned, and then he would have a ringside seat to witness the fulfillment of his prophecy. Nineveh might yet be destroyed, and with it, the impending danger to his own spiritually tepid homeland. He might yet return a hero to his own country.

Jonah's Surveillance Outpost

Jonah expected to be there for some time, likely until the city fell back into its old habits and suffered the penalty God had warned them about. He built a crude shelter

Ever get angry at God for not meeting your expectations?

and made himself comfortable. It did not provide much shade, however. God made a vine grow up overnight, and it gave shade for the prophet. Jonah probably reasoned things were finally working in his favor. He was more comfortable and quite pleased about the extraordinary appearance of the vine.

However, just one day later, God caused a worm or grub to gnaw at the root of the vine causing it to wither and die just as the sun blazed hottest on Jonah's head. A scorching east wind arose causing dehydration that would inhibit the natural cooling of his body. Without the vine's additional shelter, Jonah's crude structure offered little protection from the elements. Already angry over God's response to the Ninevites' behavioral transformation, it did not take much to push him over the edge. Ever get angry at God for not meeting your expectations?

Jonah prayed again. This time he did not complain about his God problem, grounded as it was in the very character of God's self-revelation. He simply asked God to let him die. We know he was angry over the vine's demise because God asked him about his right to be angry over it. He blurted out, "I do! I am angry enough to die!"

Jonah was asked the same question, essentially, twice. Between the questions, God had acted. Yet Jonah's response was fundamentally unchanged.

The Lord Replies

The Lord's answer to Jonah was straightforward, but touched the prophet on many levels. He pointed out that Jonah had not cultivated the vine and could scarcely claim any right to its existence. It was ephemerally transient. On the other hand, the Ninevites had a large population of human beings who bore the image of God, despite their sin. Many (120,000) were young enough they did not yet know their right hand from their left. Cattle, too, were God's creation, and they were present

> *God, as Creator and Sustainer, has the ultimate right to be concerned for His whole Creation, and particularly for human beings whose souls are destined for eternity.*

in abundance within the greater district of Nineveh. God, as Creator and Sustainer, has the ultimate right to be concerned for His whole Creation, and particularly for human beings whose souls are destined for eternity, in stark contrast to the single day of the vine's existence.

Precedent: Two Questions at Mount Sinai

Only once before in the Hebrew Scriptures do we find a prophet of God asked the same question twice, with intervening action on God's part. It was to Elijah at Mount Sinai. He had just experienced the amazing victory over the hundreds of prophets of Baal at Mount Carmel. He had

called down fire from heaven and then prayed successfully for rain to break a three-year drought. Elijah then
despaired of seeing lasting national repentance. At a mere
threat from wicked queen Jezebel, he ran *to*, not *from*, God.
His purpose, however, was to tender his resignation, as
it were, at the very spot that God had first revealed His
Name to Moses. The same Name Jonah would later quote
as the reason for his original flight from the presence of
God to renounce his calling as a herald of the King of kings.

When he arrived, the Hebrew text tells us that he went
into *the* cave and spent the night. The definite article is significant. Only one other place in the Bible mentions a cave
(or crevasse or rocky cleft) on Mount Sinai: it is the place,
symbolic of Christ, where God covered Moses while His
goodness passed before him and God proclaimed His Name:

> *The LORD, The LORD, the compassionate and gra-
> cious God, slow to anger, abounding in love and
> faithfulness, maintaining love to thousands, and for-
> giving wickedness, rebellion, and sin. Yet he does not
> leave the guilty unpunished; he punishes the chil-
> dren and their children for the sin of the fathers to
> the third and fourth generation.* (Exodus 34:6-7).

The problem Elijah had with God was he had been
zealous, but it seemed for naught. What was God doing
to vindicate His own covenant? Elijah was twice asked

by God, "What are you doing here, Elijah?" Elijah had deserted his station and wanted to die, as Jonah also later wanted to do when God did not do things the way the prophet wanted Him to. Elijah thought he was the last of his line (although he should have known better; Obadiah had told him he had hidden a hundred of God's prophets from slaughter by wicked King Ahab).[31]

Between the two questions directed by God to Elijah, God acted. First, by a mighty rock-shattering wind; next, by a great earthquake; finally, by fire. God was in none of them. Earthquake, wind, and fire had accompanied God's manifestation of His holy presence on Mount Sinai when He gave Moses the Law. But it was the still small voice that Elijah recognized and that moved him to stand, face covered in reverence, at the mouth of the cave. God had said to Moses that no man living could look upon His face and survive.

> God's saving purposes do not ultimately rest on any single person other than the promised Messiah, the anointed Son of David.

It was only then, with Elijah standing in the Lord's presence in the mouth of the cave, that God answered Elijah's complaint. Elijah's resignation was not accepted; he must retrace his steps and resume his assigned station. God's work would not flicker out with Elijah's passing. He would anoint a new king over Damascus and a new king over Israel. Most important, He would anoint a successor to Elijah in the person of Elisha.

God would chasten His wayward people with the sword of a resurgent Syria. He would eradicate the dynasty of wicked King Ahab and his Baal-worshiping Sidonian consort Jezebel. He would continue His chastening of the false religionists within Israel through the work of Elisha. God's saving purposes do not ultimately rest on any single person other than the promised Messiah, the anointed Son of David. God told Elijah that He had preserved, not one hundred, but seven thousand who remained faithful to the Lord. So, let's return now to God's response to Jonah.

Last Call to Israel

The little book of Jonah is the only one in the entire Bible that ends with a question:

"Should I not be concerned about that great city?"

The narrative leaves the question without response from the prophet. The question is both a statement about the wideness of God's mercy to the nations and, at the same time, a pointed indictment of Jonah's flawed sense of priorities.

It is sometimes suggested that Jonah could not have written the book, because no ancient writer would write so self-critically. That is precisely the point, of course. Jonah himself was convicted by God's work around, through, and finally within him. God is sovereign. He will work in us, through us, and around us to accomplish His will both for us and others!

That Jonah wrote the book (or dictated it for his assistant to do so as the prophet Jeremiah would later do with Baruch)[32] is the testament to his having grasped the lesson. That it was received by Israel as God's written Word, together with the other Hebrew Scriptures up to that time, is evidence that its full purpose included a challenge to Israel itself. The book constitutes a last call to God's people in the northern kingdom of Israel.

Unrepentant, the people of the northern kingdom persisted in their sins, provoking the holiness of God. His patience would endure for only one last generation. Perhaps exactly (but certainly close to) forty years following Jonah's experience and authoring his book, Samaria would be surrounded and besieged. The capital of Israel would fall, and all of the ten tribes of the northern kingdom, apart from a remnant who would escape to the southern kingdom of Judah, would be carried captive by their conquerors. Transplanted and absorbed into

> *God is sovereign. He will work in us, through us, and around us to accomplish His will both for us and others!*

a mélange of other foreign peoples, they ceased to exist as an identifiable community. The conquering empire would be Assyria. Nineveh had returned from the brink of disintegration to become once more a world-dominating, ruthlessly cruel and efficient, war machine. Hosea's prophecy was fulfilled, and Jonah's fear was realized.

Consider This...

Jonah himself was convicted by God's work around, through, and finally within him. That he wrote the book is the testament to his having grasped the lesson.

Have you been able to grasp the lesson given you in this little book by Jonah? Write it down in your own words:

_____

The question God asked at the end of this book is both a statement about the wideness of God's mercy to the nations and, at the same time, a pointed indictment of Jonah's flawed sense of priorities.

Have you ever questioned God's reasons for blessing others instead of you, or not punishing them and rewarding you when you have faithfully served Him?

In what areas of your life are you questioning God right now?

Act Upon This...

It is sometimes suggested that Jonah could not have written the book, because no writer would write so self-critically. That is precisely the point, of course.

Are you willing to be painfully self-critical and brutally honest about your attitude towards completing the mission and purpose God has called you to complete?

Write down the mission and purpose in this season of your life that God has called you to complete:

_____.

Write down the excuses or hindrances you are experiencing that keep you from moving across the finish line:

_____.

Are you ready to stop comparing yourself to others and do what God has called you to do and leave the others to Him and His mercy and plan?

If so, what are your next steps of obedience?

_____

If not, when will you repent and do what's required of you by God?

Chapter Six

THE SIGN OF JONAH

The Sign of Jonah

Then some of the Pharisees and teachers of the law said to him,

"Teacher, we want to see a miraculous sign from you."

He answered, "A wicked and adulterous generation asks for a miraculous sign!

But none will be given it except the sign of the prophet Jonah.

For as Jonah was three days and three nights in the belly of a huge fish,

so the Son of Man will be three days and three nights in the heart of the earth.

The men of Nineveh will stand up at the judgment with this generation and condemn it;

*for they repented at the preaching of Jonah, and now
one greater than Jonah is here.* (Matthew 12:38–41)

Nearly eight centuries after Jonah's day, another Jewish preacher would grow up near Jonah's hometown of Gath-Hepher in Galilee. Jesus' early ministry was mostly centered around the Sea of Galilee. Since His birth in Bethlehem and His early childhood sojourn in Egypt, He had been raised in Nazareth, which means "branch" or "sprout." It was a "sprout town" established by Jews returning from exile in Babylon nearly five centuries earlier in fulfillment of Isaiah's prophecy, "A shoot will come up from the stump of Jesse; from his roots a Branch will bear fruit."[34]

Jesus was Himself the personal embodiment of the Branch, "He shall be called a Nazarene."[35] The Hebrew word for "Branch" used by Isaiah and the words Nazareth and Nazarene share a common root. Jesus' itinerant ministry was frequently challenged by leaders of the religious establishment whose hypocrisy His life and teaching laid bare.

On a superficial reading, Jesus' interlocutors' question in Matthew 12:38 may seem innocent enough to us, but it is not. Were they in good faith simply seeking to authenticate His ministry? The immediately preceding context of the account given by Matthew in chapter twelve gives a very different picture.

Jesus and Beelzebub

Then they brought him a demon-possessed man who was blind and mute, and Jesus healed him, so that he could both talk and see.

All the people were astonished and said, "Could this be the Son of David?"

But when the Pharisees heard this, they said, "It is only by Beelzebub, the prince of demons, that this fellow drives out demons."

Jesus knew their thoughts and said to them, "Every kingdom divided against itself will be ruined, and every city or household divided against itself will not stand.

If Satan drives out Satan, he is divided against himself. How then can his kingdom stand?

And if I drive out demons by Beelzebub, by whom do your people drive them out?

So then, they will be your judges. But if I drive out demons by the Spirit of God, then the kingdom of God has come upon you.

"Or again, how can anyone enter a strong man's house and carry off his possessions

unless he first ties up the strong man? Then he can rob his house.

"He who is not with me is against me, and he who does not gather with me scatters.

*And so I tell you, every sin and blasphemy will be
forgiven men,*

*but the blasphemy against the Spirit will not be
forgiven.*

*Anyone who speaks a word against the Son of Man
will be forgiven,*

*but anyone who speaks against the Holy Spirit will
not be forgiven,*

either in this age or in the age to come.

*"Make a tree good and its fruit will be good, or make
a tree bad and its fruit will be bad,*

for a tree is recognized by its fruit.

*You brood of vipers, how can you who are evil say
anything good?*

For out of the overflow of the heart the mouth speaks.

*The good man brings good things out of the good
stored up in him,*

*and the evil man brings evil things out of the evil
stored up in him.*

*But I tell you that men will have to give account on
the day of judgment*

for every careless word they have spoken.

*For by your words you will be acquitted, and by your
words you will be condemned."* (Matthew 12:22-37)

Jesus' opponents had witnessed miracle after authen-
ticating miracle. He had fed the multitudes, healed the

sick, cast out demons, and even raised the dead. Yet in each instance, their response had been, in effect: "That does not count. It does not meet our judgment criteria. His miracles are accomplished, not by God, but by the Prince of demons."

> *The greatest work of the Holy Spirit is to point to Jesus. The unpardonable sin, Jesus said, is the final rejection of the Spirit's testimony to Jesus.*

Miracles do not happen willy-nilly in the Bible or in history. Neither do prophetic and apostolic revelation. They tend to occur in clusters or bursts, and the bursts of revelation and of miracles correlate with one another, as Geerhardos Vos observed, in a "word-deed-word" pattern of authentication.[36]

Nicodemus could honestly say to Jesus, "We know that you are a teacher who has come from God, because no one could perform the miraculous signs you are doing if God were not with him."[37] Jesus himself declared, "Do not believe me unless I do what my Father does. But if I do it, even though you do not believe me, believe the miracles, that you may know and understand that the Father is in me, and I in the Father."[38]

Another New Testament writer declares, "God also testified to it [*i.e.*, salvation in Jesus Christ] by signs, wonders, and various miracles, and gifts of the Holy Spirit distributed according to his will."[39] Jesus' miracles were never done simply for their own sake. They always pointed to salvation through faith in Him.

Jesus gave a stern warning to those who refused to acknowledge the work of the Spirit of God (v.28), but resisted it instead, even to the point of ascribing the work of the Spirit of God to the devil himself (v.24). The greatest work of the Holy Spirit is to point to Jesus.[40] The unpardonable sin, Jesus said, is the final rejection of the Spirit's testimony to Jesus.[41]

If we are fearful of having committed the unpardonable sin, and desire instead to come to Christ in repentance and faith, we may be confident that we have not committed that sin. Only the Spirit of God can cause us to turn to Christ, and if we desire to come to Him, He has said it is only because His Father has drawn us.[42] He has promised never to turn away those who come in faith to Him.[43]

"No Sign But . . ."

To those who demanded a miraculous sign from Him, Jesus replied, "A wicked and adulterous generation asks for a miraculous sign! But none will be given it except the sign of the prophet Jonah."[44] He went on to declare:

"For as Jonah was three days and three nights in the belly of a huge fish, so the Son of Man will be three days and three nights in the heart of the earth. The men of Nineveh will stand up at the judgment with this generation and

condemn it; for they repented at the preaching of Jonah, and now one greater than Jonah is here." (Matthew 12:40-41)

Jesus was clearly speaking of His death and resurrection, the focal point of His ministry as champion-redeemer (Hebrew, *goel*) of His people. The Apostle Paul would later write that the death, burial, and resurrection of Jesus Christ are the heart of the Gospel and of "first importance."[45]

For those whose hardened hearts rejected every witness to the saving work of Jesus Christ, there would be but one—ultimate—sign: not a sign that they would judge, but one that would judge *them*. The northern kingdom of Israel had been swept away only a generation after their "last call" through Jonah. One generation after Jesus' death and resurrection, the Jewish religious leaders and all those who had rejected Him were swept away by the invading Roman armies under Titus in AD 70. Jerusalem and the Temple were completely destroyed just as He predicted.

A Greater Than Jonah

It is tempting to see the symbolic experience of Jonah in the sea creature's craw as only superficially parallel to Jesus' own at Calvary and Gethsemane. After all, Jonah was rebellious and was subjected to the consequences of his own sin. Jesus was the sinless Lamb of God who came to take away the sin of the world.[46] Jonah did not actually die and even considered his being swallowed by the monster

as a rescue, though with the anticipation of full restoration to worship at God's Temple. Jesus, by contrast,
actually underwent true physical death and
resurrection.

> *Jesus went through
> death, experienced
> hell, total separation
> from God, and in His
> human nature as the
> Person of Jesus Christ,
> He underwent the three
> hours of darkness and
> silence during His total
> of six hours of suffering
> on the cross.*

But that is just the
point. In his rebellion,
Jonah was very much
representative of Israel
in the nation's viola-
tion of God's covenant
and resistance to God's
grace and calling. Jonah,
like God's people Israel,
deserved to die. Jesus,
of course, did not. At His
baptism, Jesus identified
with His people in their
lostness. John the Baptizer had at first recoiled from bap-
tizing Jesus, and with good reason, saying: "I need to be
baptized by you, and do you come to me?"[47] Jesus replied,
"Let it be so now; it is proper for us to do this to fulfill all
righteousness."[48]

In His explanation of the Gospel to Nicodemus, Jesus
said, "Just as Moses lifted up the snake in the desert, so
the Son of Man must be lifted up, that everyone who
believes in him may have eternal life."[49] The serpent is
most frequently a symbol of Satan, our great malevolent

adversary. How could Jesus compare Himself with a serpent? It is because He came to identify with His people and become their substitute, taking the punishment due to them upon Himself. Water baptism, like Noah's flood, represents judgment and renewal,[50] and Jesus underwent water baptism as an identification with His people.[51] It is as if He had said, "Father, your people have indeed sinned against you and have brought upon themselves the judgment of death. I am with them, and for them. Let the punishment due to them fall upon me instead."

The Apostle Paul tells us, "God made him who had no sin to be sin for us, so that in him we might become the righteousness of God."[52] Jesus went through death, experienced hell, total separation from God, and in His human nature as the Person of Jesus Christ, He underwent the three hours of darkness and silence during His total of six hours of suffering on the cross.

"He saved us, not because of righteous things we had done, but because of his mercy. He saved us through the washing of rebirth and renewal by the Holy Spirit, whom he poured out on us generously through Jesus Christ our Savior, so that, having been justified by his grace, we might become heirs having the hope of eternal life." (Titus 3:5-7)

It is Jesus' death and resurrection that empowers the believer then and now:

"If we live, we live to the Lord; and if we die, we die to the Lord. So, whether we live or die, we belong to the Lord. For this very reason, Christ died and returned to life so that he might be the Lord of both the dead and the living." (Romans 14:8-9)

Jesus is indeed a "greater than Jonah." What Jonah's life and experience pointed toward, Jesus perfectly fulfilled.

Consider This...

Jesus went through death, experienced hell, total separation from God, and in His human nature as the Person of Jesus Christ, He underwent the three hours of darkness and silence during His total of six hours of suffering on the cross.

Read John 3:16-18.

What does this passage mean to you personally? Write down how this passage speaks to your life?

_____.

Act Upon This...

Read John 6:37-44. Only the Spirit of God can cause us to turn to Christ, and if we desire to come to Him, He has said it is only because His Father has drawn us, and

He has promised never to turn away those who come in faith to Him.

Do you hear the Spirit of God calling you to turn to Christ?

Do you desire to come to Him?
Will you receive His promise today?
Read Romans 10:9.

Do you believe in your heart that Jesus died for your sins on that cross and that God raised Jesus from the dead so that you could be saved from death and hell?

Will you confess your sins, confess Jesus as your Lord, and receive His gift of eternal life?

Are you willing to stop doing what is wrong in your life and start trusting Jesus through the Scriptures and the Holy Spirit to empower you to make right decisions and obey God? If so, write a prayer telling this to God:

———————————————————————

———————————————————————

EPILOGUE

J onah is more than a fanciful and colorful character in a children's storybook. He is a crucial hinge point in redemptive history, a living illustration of the two sides of God's covenant: blessing and cursing. As such, he points to Jesus, who took His people's judgment in order to give them His righteousness, and with it, new life in Him. That transaction is the Great Exchange whereby we receive God's free gift of forgiveness and salvation.

Two Sides of God's Covenant

No sooner had the first human beings transgressed against God's commandment in the Garden of Eden, we find God giving a gracious promise of a coming Savior. God pronounced judgment upon their sin, but first said to the deceiving serpent: "Cursed are you . . . and I will put enmity between you and the woman, and between your offspring and hers; he will crush your head, and you will strike his heel."[53]

There can be but two sides in the cosmic conflict of redemptive history: God's and Satan's. The serpent had accused God of stinginess and of holding back Adam and Eve from becoming like God. By implication, the serpent posed as on their side versus God's side. God's judgment on the serpent spoke of returning the enmity to its proper boundary. To be at war with Satan is to be aligned with God. **There is no third side.** The seed of the woman foretold by God would be born in due time. He would be laid in a manger and grow up identifying with all the poverty and oppression experienced by His people.

God's call to Abraham was unmerited. He was raised in an idolatrous pagan home, and he was a Gentile Mesopotamian Semite from what was one of the last and strongest centers of Sumerian occult culture in Ur of the Chaldees. He was commanded to leave his relatives and his city and go to a land unknown to him. His call would likewise include reference to blessing and cursing:

> *"I will make you into a great nation, and I will bless you; I will make your name great, and you will be a blessing. I will bless those who bless you, and whoever curses you I will curse; and all peoples on earth will be blessed through you."* (Genesis 12:2-3)

Abraham was blessed to be a blessing.

God brought the Hebrew slaves, Abraham's descendants, out of Egypt and established His covenant with them at Sinai and did so again on the east of Jordan. He sealed it with promises of blessing for faith and obedience and cursing for unbelief and disobedience.[54] Judgment upon the nations would bring blessing to Israel, but only if Israel remained faithful to the God of the covenant.

After the promised Messiah had come, the Apostle Paul would write that judgment upon Israel was the occasion for God's fulfillment of His promise to bring blessing to the nations:

Again I ask: Did they stumble so as to fall beyond recovery? Not at all! Rather, because of their transgression, salvation has come to the Gentiles to make Israel envious. [12] But if their transgression means riches for the world, and their loss means riches for the Gentiles, how much greater riches will their fullness bring! I am talking to you Gentiles. Inasmuch as I am the apostle to the Gentiles, I make much of my ministry in the hope that I may somehow arouse my own people to envy and save some of them. For if their rejection is the reconciliation of the world, what will their acceptance be but life from the dead?
(Romans 11:11-15)

Israel's final restoration brings the ultimate blessing: life from the dead. The resurrection of Jesus Christ forms the foundation for Paul's confidence in the fulfillment of the promise.

Implications for God's People

For all who repent and believe the Good News of salvation in Jesus Christ as Redeemer and Lord, there are implications. God has chosen us in Christ not simply for our own blessedness, but also for the purpose of being His instruments of blessing to others. The Christian life is fundamentally a life for others. *To be in Christ is to be with Him in God's mission to the world.*

> *God has chosen us in Christ not simply for our own blessedness, but also for the purpose of being His instruments of blessing to others. The Christian life is fundamentally a life for others.*

Israel was always intended to be a light to the nations, a missional and pilgrim people. We who are Christ's today are to be no less (rather, even more) missional. We, too, are a pilgrim people, strangers and aliens in the world, carrying by word and life the Good News that Jesus Christ is Lord. We who were not a people are now the people of God; we who had not received mercy have now received mercy.[55] An unfaithful Church will find she still is an instrument for the outworking of God's missional purpose through her chastening. A faithful Church will find her Lord is faithful to His promise to be with her to the consummation of the age.

The call to covenant union with Jesus Christ is a call to worship, obedience, and missional service—sharing the Good News of Jesus Christ with others. We are called to reach out to those around us, near and far, including those unlike us and the unlovely. We were loved by God when we were still aliens and enemies. Now we are to demonstrate that same grace toward others.

Earthquake, wind, and fire attended God's giving of Israel's covenant charter to Moses at Mount Sinai, with the proclamation of His Name. Earthquake, wind, and fire preceded the still, small voice of God to Elijah from the same mountain. It would not be the spectacularly visible, but the far more powerful, invisible work of God that would be the mightiest miracle of all. It is the bringing of life to the spiritually dead[56] and the changing of hearts of stone to hearts of flesh,[57] living and throbbing in resonance with God's own.

Indeed, earthquake, wind, and fire would at last attend the disciples of the Galilean carpenter as they gathered on another mountain, Zion, not in a cave, but in an upper room.[58] Pentecostal power would fall upon them, and they would boldly proclaim the Good News of salvation in the Name of the risen Lord Jesus. Jesus had said that they would do greater works than He had done during His public ministry, yet the book of Acts records comparatively few.

Three possible explanations are:

1) Jesus was mistaken (yet His disciples had full confidence in Him, a fact that appears to be inconsistent with the notion of Jesus' fallibility in the matter).

2) Far more and greater miracles were performed and simply omitted in writing the book of Acts and in the epistles than had been omitted in the writing of the Gospels.

3) The greatest miracle of all was the movement of the Spirit of God across entire cities and people groups, bringing throngs to saving faith in Him and equipping every member of the believing community with mutually-complementing spiritual gifts, something that Jesus in His earthly ministry did not witness.

Of the three, the last explanation is arguably the most natural, for the book of Acts contains the acts of the risen Christ by the power of the Holy Spirit through His apostles and His Church.[59] *But the way to Pentecost had first to pass through Calvary and the Garden Tomb*, our Lord's death and resurrection. Only the single Great Hero of the grand narrative of the Bible, the "one greater than Jonah," could ever accomplish it.

The Church today stands between Pentecost and our Lord's return at the close of history.[60] The risen Christ came to seek and to save that which was lost,[61] saying, "As the Father has sent me, I am sending you."[62] The task of missions is not optional. It may be, and often is, costly, but it will most certainly be worth the cost. Eternity in the presence of our Savior, surrounded by an innumerable host of those who, like us, were called out of darkness into His wonderful light, will cause all trials in this life to pale in comparison.[63]

The resurrection power of the Lord Jesus Christ, *one greater than Jonah*, guarantees it.

Consider This...

God has chosen us in Christ not simply for our own blessedness, but also for the purpose of being His instruments of blessing to others. The Christian life is fundamentally a life for others.

How is your life a reflection of Jesus Christ the risen Savior? _____

How are you an instrument of blessing to others? Describe: _____

Act Upon This...

We are called to reach out to those around us, near and far, including those unlike us and the unlovely. The task of missions is not optional.

What does the task of missions mean to you personally?

_____

Read Luke 19:10. *Make a list of those who do not know Jesus in your relationships:*

_____

_____

_____

When will you pray for them to know Christ as Lord and Savior?

_____

_____

_____

When will you share with them the Gospel?

_____

_____

_____

Read John 20:21.

*What is Jesus saying to you today?*_____

_____

Read Acts 2:38.

Have you asked for and received the empowerment of His Holy Spirit to equip you to do the work He has called you to do? _____

Are you ready to go and do what God has called you to do in this generation? _____

Will you share this book with your pastor and other church leaders and encourage them to use this book as a study guide for a class or small group? _____

_____

_____

Write a prayer asking God through His Spirit to embolden you to share the Gospel of Jesus Christ in your family, at work, in your church and community:

_____

_____

_____

FOR FURTHER READING

Ferguson, Sinclair. 2008. *Man Overboard! The Story of Jonah*. Carlyle, PA: The Banner of Truth Trust.

Robertson, O. Palmer. 1990. *Jonah: A Study in Compassion*. Carlyle, PA: The Banner of Truth Trust.

Timmer, Daniel C. 2011. *A Gracious and Compassionate God: Mission, Salvation, and Spirituality in the Book of Jonah*. Downers Grove, IL: InterVarsity Press.

ENDNOTES

J esus spoke of the very smallest letters and calligraphy marks that distinguish one letter from another as all being inviolate (Matt. 5:18; Luke 16:17).

[2] See *Biblical Inerrancy: The Historical Evidence* by Norman Geisler (2013).

[3] Deut. 18:21-22; 2 Cor. 12:12; Heb. 2:4.

[4] Lk. 24:44

[5] Lk 24:27

[6] Matt. 9:36; Jn. 10:16; Matt. 28:19-20

[7] Isaiah 36.

[8] See, for example, Psalm 55:6 and Hosea 7:11.

[9] 1 Kings 21:22-29.

[10] 2 Kings 10:30.

[11] 2 Kings 10:31-33.

[12] 2 Kings 14:23-29.

[13] Hosea 9:3.

[14] See, for example, 2 Kings 11:1.

15 Archer, Gleason. 1974. A Survey of Old Testament Introduction. Chicago: Moody Press.

16 Exodus 33:18-34:7 and 1 Kings 19

17 Joshua 7

18 Mark 4:35-41

19 Mark 4:41

20 Isaiah 65:24

21 Matthew 1:21

22 Jonah 4:2

23 W.W. Hallo, "From Qarqar to Carchemish: Assyria and Israel in the light of new discoveries," BAR 2 (1975) 152-188.

24 Jeremiah 18:7-8

25 Mark 10:12-16

26 John 2:12-17 and Luke 19:45-46

27 John 2:17

28 Exodus 4:14

29 Psalm 7:11, KJV

30 Ephesians 4:26

31 1 Kings 19

32 1 Kings 18:13

33 Jeremiah 36:4

34 Isaiah 11:1

35 Matthew 2:23

36 Geerharos Vos, *Biblical Theology: Old and New Testaments*, 1975.

37 John 3:2

[38] John 10:37-38

[39] Hebrews 2:4

[40] John 15:26 and 16:14

[41] Matthew 12:31-32

[42] John 6:44

[43] John 6:37

[44] Matthew 12:39

[45] 1 Corinthians 15:1-4

[46] John 1:29

[47] Matthew 3:14

[48] Matthew 3:15

[49] John 3:14-15

[50] 1 Peter 3:18-22

[51] 1 Peter 3:18

[52] 2 Corinthians 5:21

[53] Genesis 3:15

[54] Deuteronomy 28

[55] 1 Peter 2:10

[56] Ezekiel 37

[57] Ezekiel 36:25-27

[58] Acts 2:2-3 and 4:31

[59] Acts 1:1-2 and 1:8

[60] Titus 2:13

[61] Luke 19:10

[62] John 20:21

[63] Revelation 7:9-12; Romans 8:18

ABOUT THE AUTHOR

S am Larsen, D.Min., Ph.D., has served as a U.S. Navy Chaplain, missionary, and missions professor. He and Louise, his wife of forty-five years, live in the metro Atlanta area where Sam continues in his "retirement" to write, to teach classes, and to speak at missions conferences. He can be contacted at SamLarsen.global@att.net or at Dr. Samuel Larsen, 3330 Cobb Parkway Suite 324-242, Acworth, GA 30101.

Additional copies of this book may be ordered from Xulon Press through local bookstores or on BarnesandNoble.com or Amazon.com as well as at seminars, classes, or conferences at which Dr. Larsen speaks, or from Dr. Larsen at the postal address above. Net proceeds from the sale of the book are entirely dedicated to the work of global missions.

ENDORSEMENTS

Our great God not only saves us, but He calls us to glorify Him by proclaiming His Word. In spite of our weaknesses and through His power, He accomplishes His will for the nations through human vessels. Rarely has this been as powerfully manifested as it was in the life of Jonah. In *Gripped by a Global God* Sam Larsen leads us on a journey into Jonah's story and helps us to see God's working in our own. Engaging, accessible, and applicable, Larsen has given every believer a gift in *Gripped by a Global God*. I encourage you to dig into the life of Jonah and consider what it might mean for you to be gripped by the same God who took hold of him.

M. David Sills, D.Miss, Ph.D.
A.P. and Faye Stone Chair of Christian Missions and Cultural Anthropology
Director of Global Strategic Initiatives and Intercultural Programs
Southern Seminary, Louisville, Kentucky

Many think they know the book of Jonah–an exciting story about a reluctant missionary in the Old Testament. Sam Larsen, a sailor turned missionary theologian shows Jonah to be more than an exciting story. Dr. Larsen knows you can't escape from God. As he unfolds the story of Jonah he shows how the reluctant missionary points to Jesus the willing Savior.

Dr. Allen Curry
Interim Pastor, Proclamation Presbyterian Church,
Bryn Mawr, Pennsylvania
Professor Emeritus of Christian Education
Reformed Theological Seminary

Gripped by a Global God is an intriguing assessment of this first biblical biographical missions case study of Jonah! What was Jonah's problem? Did he ever "get" God's agenda? How did Jonah's plight fit in with the rest of God's agenda? Larsen's creative narrative addresses these questions and more. Each chapter concludes with things to consider and things to act upon. And yes, Larsen connects the dots of *Jonah* with those of Jesus and today's mission of God. Well-done Dr. Larsen!

Dr. Michael Barnett
Dean, College of Intercultural Studies
Columbia International University

I am very impressed by the book's balance: its biblical exposition is solid and nuanced, its tone is warmly pastoral, and its passion for bringing all of life into the pursuit of God's glory and the good of others through the Gospel is evident everywhere. Perhaps what struck me most was the incisive, pastoral orientation of the questions at the chapter-ends. They remind me of what I think is among the best of Christian spirituality (Diary of Private Prayer by Baillie; Packer's various works on holiness)—intentionally, deliberately, slowly working on one's heart in God's presence through his word. I hope it is widely read, prayed over, and used by God!

Daniel Timmer, Ph.D.
Author of *A Gracious and Compassionate God: Mission, Salvation and Spirituality in the Book of Jonah*
(New Studies in Biblical Theology, Series Editor Donald A. Carson)

This little book packs a big Gospel punch! Sam Larsen has successfully navigated the theological terrain of the book of Jonah and demonstrated that God's great Gospel in Jesus Christ is a light for ALL of the nations. Those who devour this book will resonate with the experience of Ezekiel, "and it was in my mouth as sweet at honey" (Ezek 3:3).

Miles V. Van Pelt, Ph.D.
Alan Belcher Professor of Old Testament and Biblical Languages
Director, Summer Institute for Biblical Languages
Academic Dean, Jackson Campus, Reformed Theological Seminary

What a precious text to read! It really reflects the author's years of meditating and understanding of the Scriptures, his long experience in teaching and preaching on this passage, and his years of missional living under the guidance of the God of Jonah, our God. But Dr. Larsen went beyond many commentaries on the book of Jonah. He has wisely taken into consideration both the context of the prophet and of the church then and today. The "Consider this..." the "Act upon this..." at the end of each chapter are priceless. No one can read this book and remain neutral in his or her walk with the Lord Jesus Christ, to whom the book of Jonah points.

Dr. Elias Medeiros
Professor of Missions, Reformed Theological Seminary

Dr. Larsen has spent his life thinking through and personifying the issues of global mission — one of the main themes of the book of Jonah. He is, by training and temperament, ideally suited to guide us through this important Old Testament book. I commend this volume to you with a full heart, grateful that an invaluable resource on Scripture has been written to help us become the disciples God intends us to be.

Derek W. H. Thomas
Robert Strong Professor of Systematic and Pastoral Theology,
RTS Atlanta
Senior Minister, First Presbyterian Church, Columbia SC

CPSIA information can be obtained at www.ICGtesting.com
Printed in the USA
LVOW04s0028041014

407177LV00001B/1/P

9 781498 413428